Sonatinas

BOOK 4
Intermediate to
Late Intermediate

Information for Teachers

Our Succeeding with the Masters®/The Festival Collection® series continues with an exciting new Sonatina series.

The sonatina series begins with mid-elementary sonatinas and continues through to early-advanced sonatinas. Well-known sonatinas, discovered gems, and sonatinas by women composers are included. Each book begins with an historical introduction to the sonatina. Students learn about form, which will support their practice and secure their performances.

We are pleased to offer every piece in its original, complete form. Though we know that students may well learn only one movement at any given time, when students see the entire sonatina they better understand how movements complement and contrast to form a complete musical picture. This series is a great way for students to *succeed with sonatinas*!

Use the FJH Pianist's Curriculum Correlation Chart to see how the six-book *Sonatina* series and the nine-book *Etudes with Technique* series correlate with the *Succeeding with the Masters®/The Festival Collection®* books and the *Succeeding at the Piano®* method.

THE
F·J·H
MUSIC
COMPANY
I N C.
Frank J. Hackinson

Production: Frank J. Hackinson
Production Coordinators: Peggy Gallagher and Philip Groeber
Consulting Editors: Edwin McLean and Stephanie Bruning
Cover Design: Andi Whitmer
Engraving: Tempo Music Press, Inc.
Printer: Tempo Music Press, Inc.

ISBN-13: 978-1-61928-153-0

Book 4: Succeeding with the Masters®/The Festival Collection®
Sonatinas–Intermediate to Late Intermediate

Sonata-allegro Form–In Depth

The standard sonata-allegro form is one of the most important forms in Western classical music. This musical structure flourished in the Classical period and maintained its importance throughout the Romantic and Contemporary eras. Sonata-allegro form applies to a single movement of a multi-movement work. In a sonata or sonatina, the first movement is most often in sonata-allegro form. This structure is similar to ternary form (ABA), yet it is more expanded and complex. The sonata-allegro form movement has three large sections that perform specific functions.

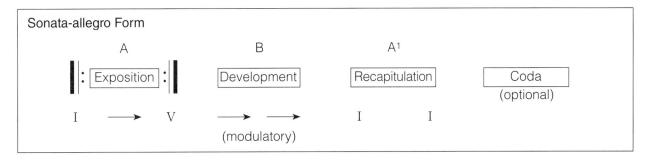

Identity of the individual sections

Exposition A

Presents one or more themes, and modulates to the dominant (or its equivalent, such as the subdominant), at which point the exposition is almost always repeated. If the exposition has a 2nd theme, it is usually presented in the dominant.

- Introduction–material that prepares the listener for what they are about to hear; establishes the key and mood of the movement.
- First theme–presents the theme in the tonic key, with a unique and individual character that will later be contrasted in style and key to the second theme.
- Transitional material–bridges the first theme to the second theme, providing a smooth transition and modulating to the new key.
- Second theme–presents a second theme, typically in a closely related key, with contrasting style and key to the first theme.
- Closing theme–concluding section of the exposition.
- The exposition is almost always repeated. Sometimes there is a first and second ending— one that leads back to the beginning, and the other that carries the movement towards the development.

Development B

"Develops" various thematic and harmonic material presented in the exposition and eventually modulates back to the tonic, which begins the recapitulation.

This section is allowed the most freedom within sonata-allegro form. The development may use the transitional material, introduction, closing material, or any of the primary themes. It is a chance for the composer to truly explore numerous possibilities contained within the musical ideas, while he/she manipulate keys, dynamics, textures, rhythms, and themes. This section is typically the most dramatic and carries a sense of unease and tension as we expectantly await the recapitulation.

Recapitulation A¹

This is a return of the A section. However, instead of modulating to the dominant, it remains in the tonic key. If there is a 2nd theme, this theme is presented in the tonic also.

Coda (optional)

This is a cadential ending to reinforce the tonality and conclude the piece.

The concluding section of the composition can range in length and depth from extended and powerful, to short and simple (codetta).

These are the most important aspects of typical sonata-allegro form. Note that the use of a 2nd theme is entirely optional—in fact, many sonatas have only one theme.

Elevation for a building with an octogonal cupola and two story pendimenting facades
from the Metropolitan Museum
Anonymous, Italian, Piedmontese, 18th century

The Classical Sonatina Versus the Romantic Sonatina

This book features sonatinas from composers living in both the Classical and Romantic eras. It is important to recognize how sonatinas maintain certain features as they develop and change in the Romantic era. In several of these compositions, characteristics from both eras are demonstrated.

Below are characteristics of both the Classical and Romantic eras.

Characteristics of the Classical Era (1750-1820)

- Melodies are elegant, graceful, and easy to sing.
- Melodies are comprised of well-balanced, symmetrical phrases.
- The simple, flowing melodies move to predictable cadences.
- Classical forms are balanced and symmetrical: binary, rounded binary, ternary, rondo, theme and variations, and sonata-allegro form.
- Short and repetitive melodic motives combine to form phrases.
- Dynamic changes contribute to the overall expression of the pieces.
- Ornamentation is used, but in a simpler style than in the Baroque era.
- Contrasts of mood show a great emotional range—moods may change suddenly within a theme or more gradually from section to section.
- There is a wide range of rhythmic possibilities, but rhythms have a regular feel, with clearly placed accents.
- Harmonies are primarily diatonic, especially favoring the tonic-dominant relationship.
- Homophonic texture is preferred over polyphonic textures.

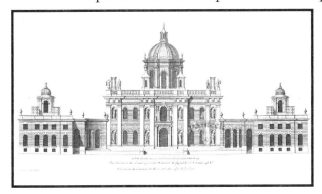

Castle Howard, front, from Vitruvius Britannicus (1720s)

Evening: Landscape with an aqueduct, 1818
Théodore Gericault (1791-1824)

Characteristics of the Romantic Era (1800-1900)

- Melodies employ chromaticism and wide leaps.
- Melodic phrases are often irregular with long, lyrical motives.
- There is greater freedom to express emotions.
- Drama is an important element of the music.
- Expression and lyricism are more important then formal structure.
- The music may employ a programmatic element (music tells a story).
- *Rubato* (fluidity of tempo) is an important expressive device.
- Greater dynamic range is used to portray varying scenes and emotions.
- Music makes greater use of tonal colors, using the full range of the keyboard.
- The harmonic vocabulary is more advanced.
- There is more variety in accompanimental patterns.
- Chords and melodies often use chromatic alterations.
- New stylized musical forms (i.e. waltz, mazurka, polonaise, etc.)
- Nationalism becomes more prevalent.

Sonatinas, Book 4 Thematics

Composer	Title	Theme	Page

8

Sonatina in G Major

Op. 300

I.

Louis Köhler
(1820-1886)

Allegro moderato (♩ = ca. 144)

L.H. legato

Fine

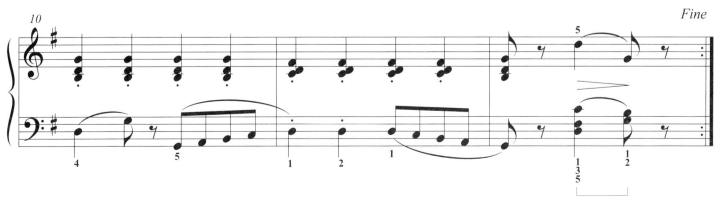

10

II.

Andante cantabile (♩ = ca. 96)

*This is a grace note; it should be played before the beat.

III.

Allegretto (♩ = ca. 104)

SONATINA IN C MAJOR

OP. 39, NO. 1

I.

I. - PRINCIPAL THEME, II. - PASSAGE, III. - PRINCIPAL THEME, IV. - CODA

Frank Lynes
(1858-1913)

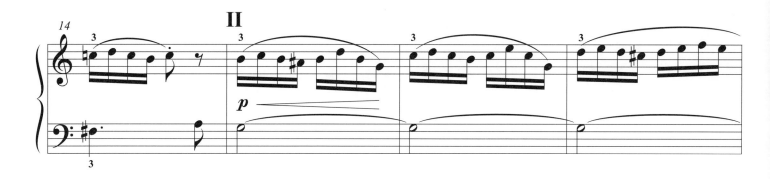

II. Minuet

Allegretto (♩ = ca. 108)

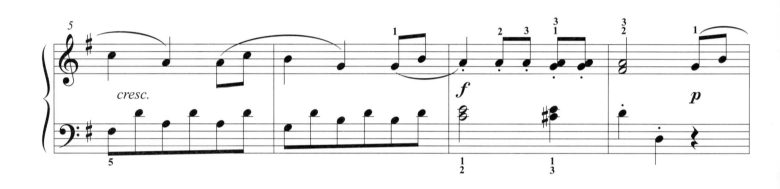

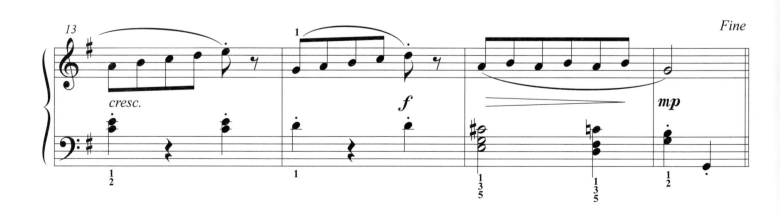

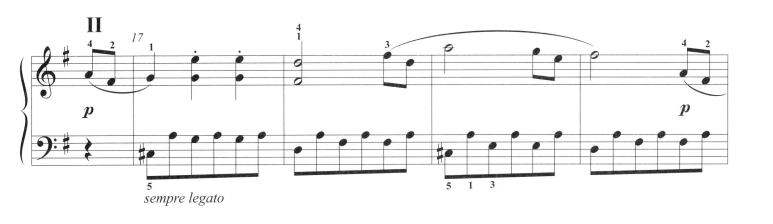

sempre legato

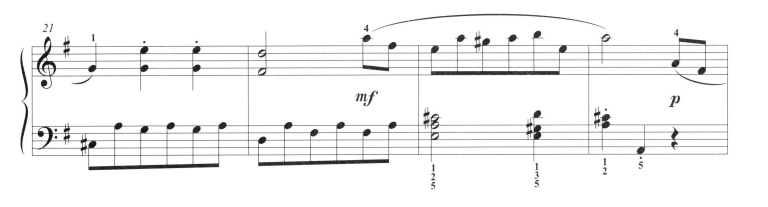

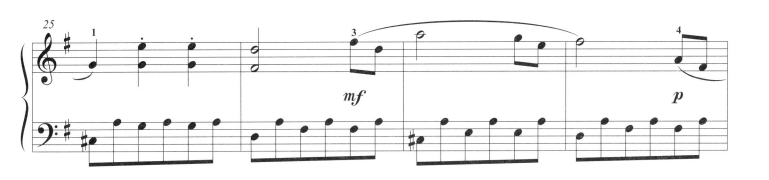

D.S. al Fine

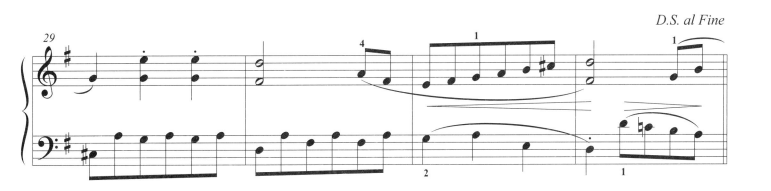

III. Allegro

Sonatina in A Minor

Op. 94, No. 4

I.

Albert Biehl
(1835-1899)

Development

II.

III.

Allegretto (♩. = ca. 80)

L.H. legato

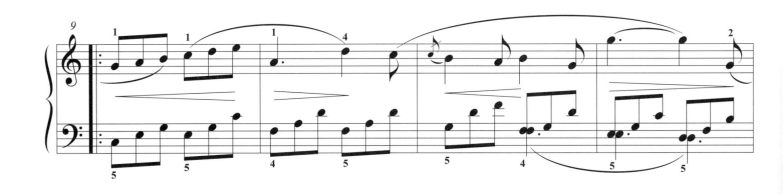

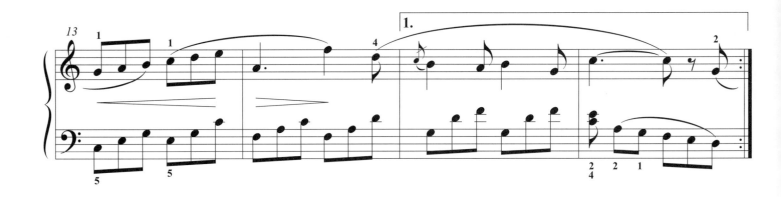

Sonatina in F Major

Anh. 5, No. 2

I.

Ludwig van Beethoven
(1770-1827)

Allegro assai (♩ = ca. 100)

II.

34

FJH2204

SONATINA NO. 6 IN D MINOR

Georg Benda
(1722-1795)

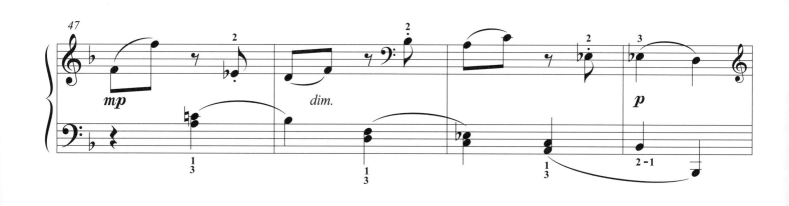

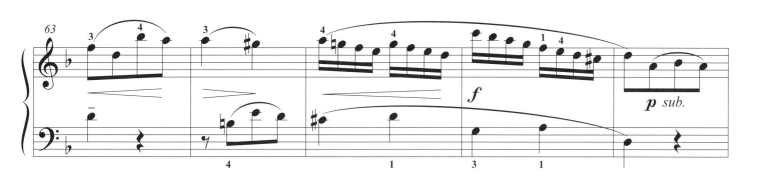

Sonatina in C Major

Op. 55, No. 1

I.

Friedrich Kuhlau
(1786-1832)

II.

48

SONATINA
OP. 136, NO. 4
I.

Carl Reinecke
(1824-1910)

Allegro moderato (♩ = ca. 126)

II. Mazurka

III.

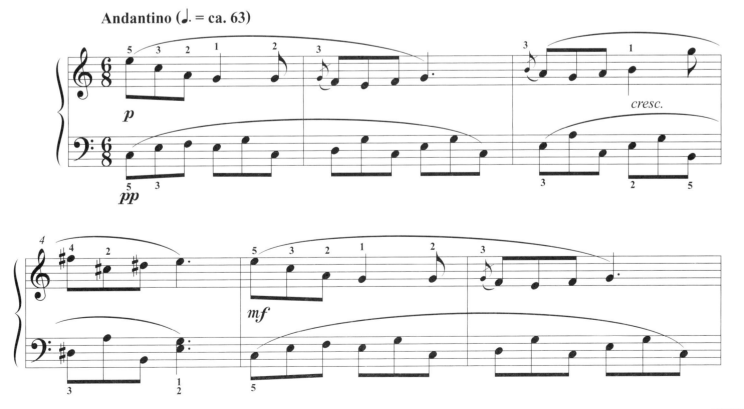

una corda

tre corde

IV.

Sonatina in F Major

Op. 4, No. 2

I.

Heinrich Lichner
(1829-1898)

Allegro moderato (♩ = ca. 144)

L.H. legato

II.

Andante sostenuto (♩ = ca. 72)

62

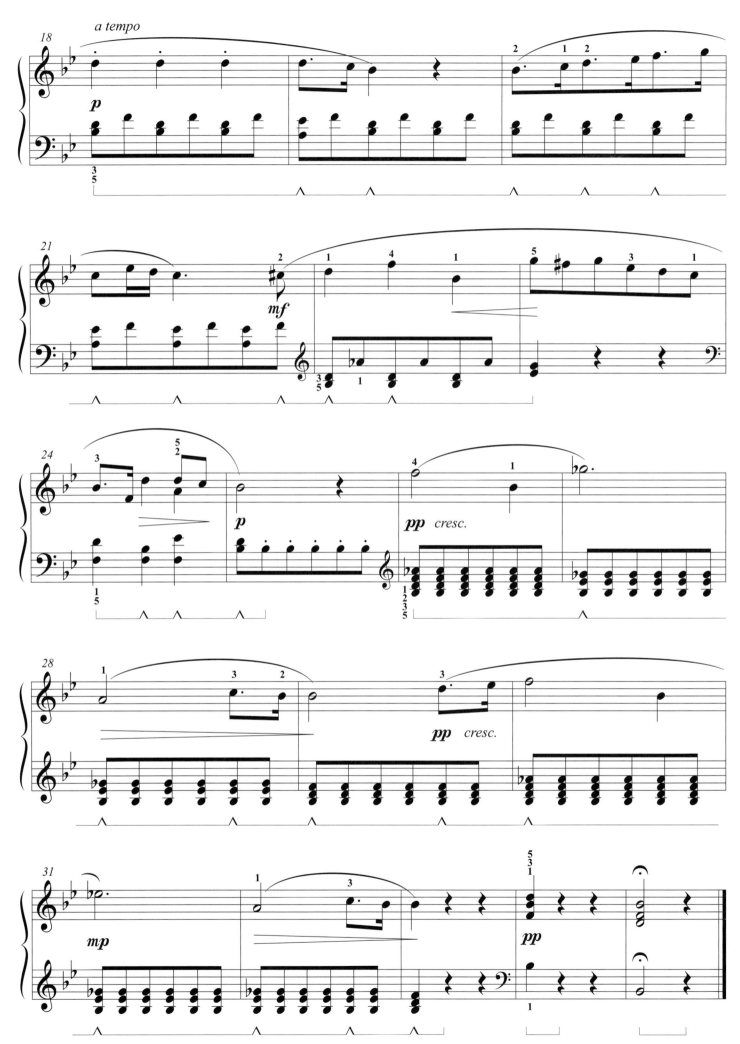

III. Polonaise

Allegro con grazia (♩ = ca. 108)

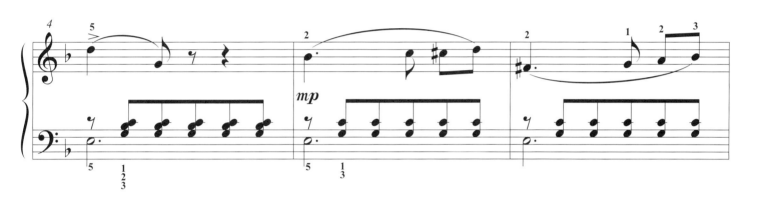

Sonatina in G Major

Op. 20, No. 1

Jan Ladislov Dussek
(1760-1812)

Allegro non tanto (♩ = 108-112)

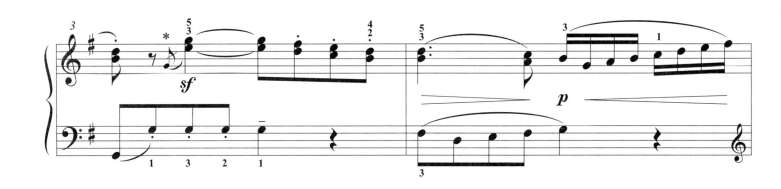

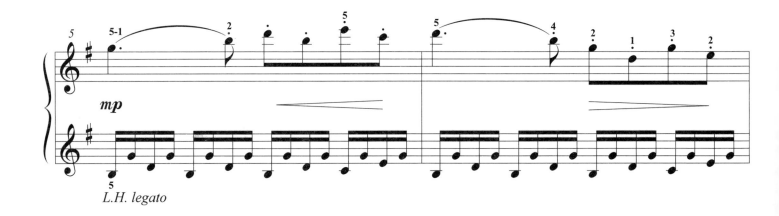

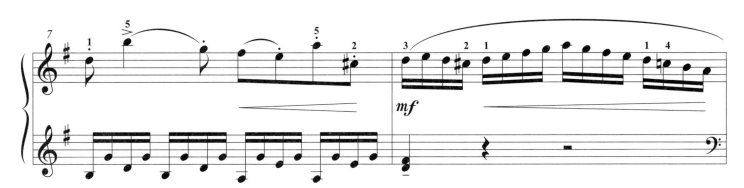

*The first movement of this sonatina is also found in The Festival Collection, Book 5.
  The grace note is omitted in some editions.

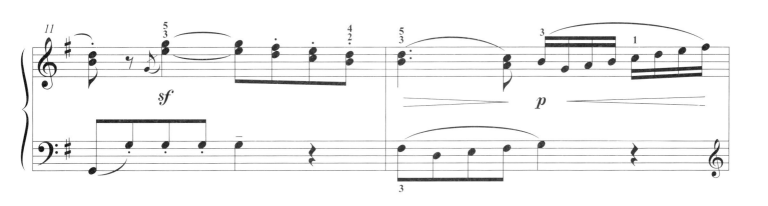

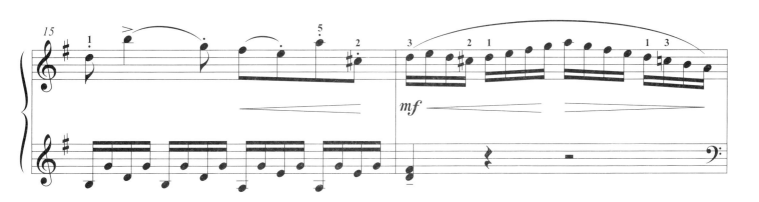

II. Rondo

Allegretto - Tempo di Minuetto (♪ = ca. 116)

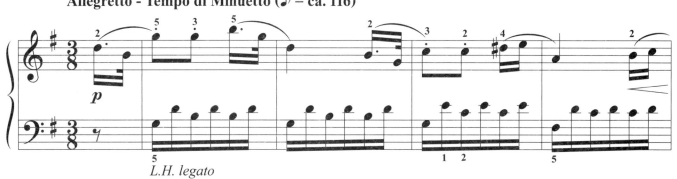

74

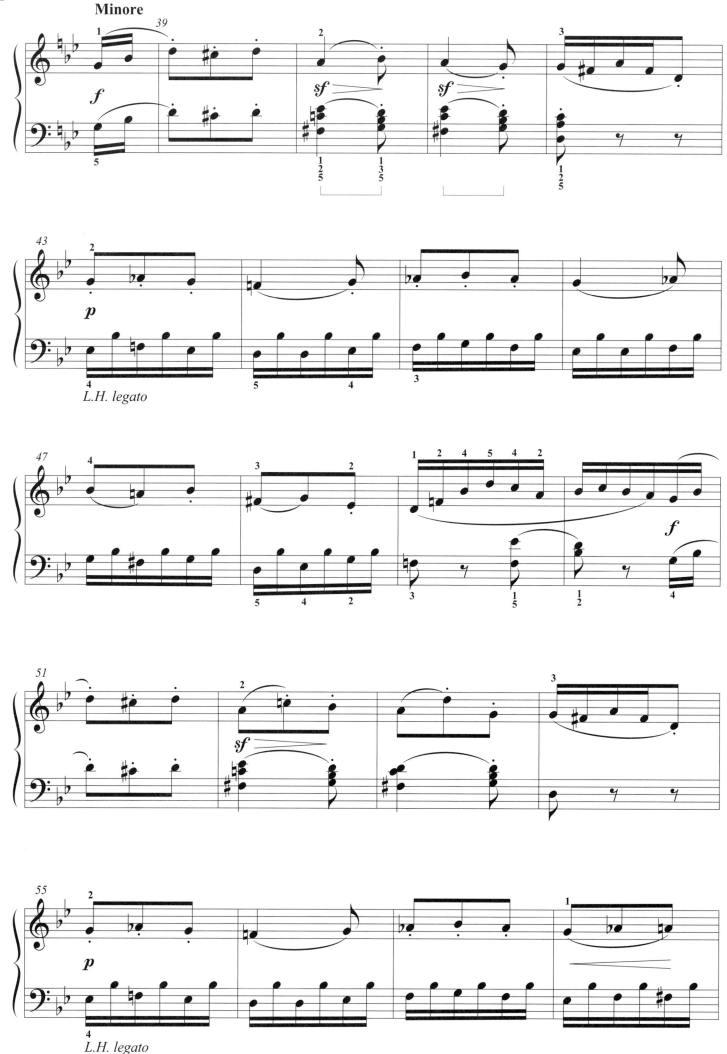

Maggiore

L.H. legato

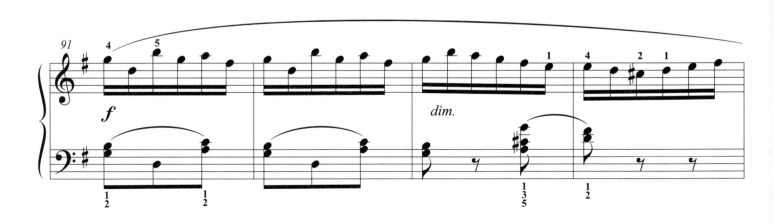

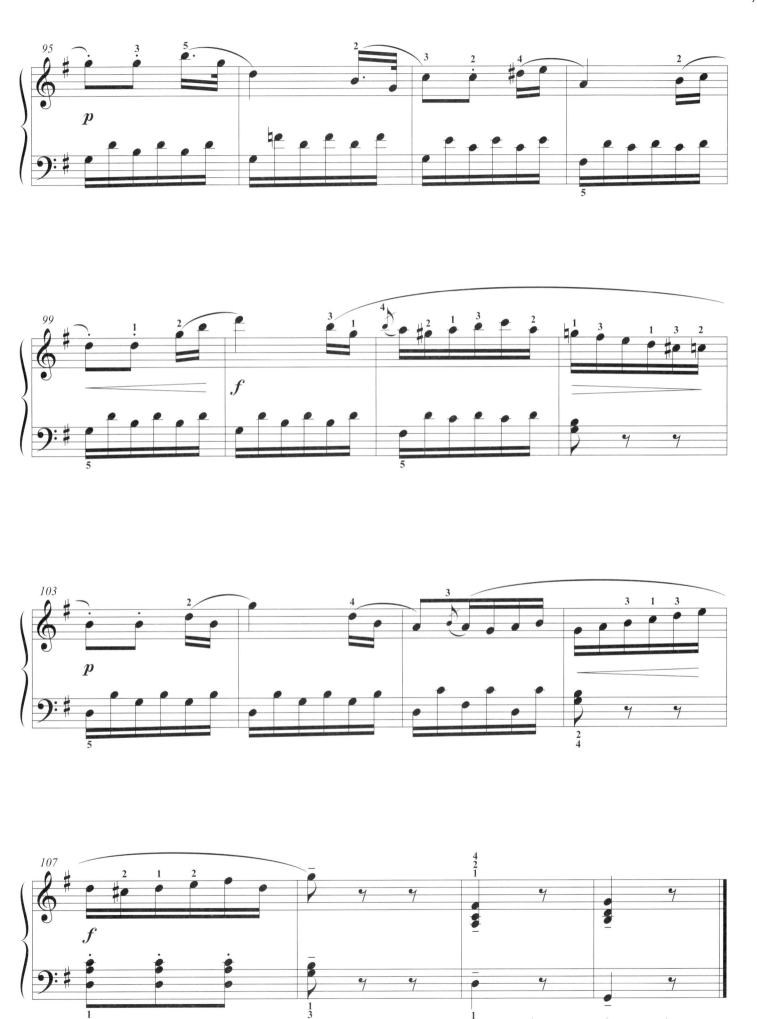

About the Pieces and Composers

Sonatina in G Major (Opus 300), by Louis Köhler (1820-1886)

Köhler began his musical career as a conductor of choral and orchestral works, but by 1847 he was completely devoted to piano teaching and pursuing his love for the piano. Today he is remembered primarily as a composer of piano compositions and collections for beginning and intermediate pianists. This sonatina is actually part of a larger collection, his *Practical Piano Method, Op. 300.* The first movement uses the relative minor rather than the more typical dominant, thus successfully manipulating both the character and key of the main theme. The second movement has a coda that uses a pedal point C, evoking the sound of a gentle heartbeat; the *Allegretto* features quick changes from *staccato* to *legato*.

Sonatina No. 1 in C Major (Opus 39, No. 1), by Frank Lynes (1858-1913)

Frank Lynes was an American composer born in Cambridge, Massachussets. Through his studies of piano, organ, and theory he realized the importance of teaching and developing strong musicianship skills at an early age. He became well known as a master pedagogue and choral director, while also producing several teaching pieces. His *Three Analytical Sonatinas for Piano, Op. 39* are written in the classical style. The main theme of the *Allegro* uses broken triads and inversions combined with quick scalar passages. A lovely *Minuet* dance movement is complemented by the lively and bright *Allegro*. Note the labeling of sections—Mr. Lynes added his own analysis to this sonatina.

Sonatina in A Minor (Opus 94, No. 4), by Albert Biehl (1835-1899)

Albert Biehl was a German composer whose works for piano include advanced technical exercises and duets. He is also known for creating educational works such as this sonatina. This sonatina is in the key of A minor and maintains the fast-slow-fast form of a typical sonatina; however, each movement strays from standard forms and characters. Minor sonorities portray a variety of emotions in this piece. Notice how the first movement contrasts a lyrical minor sound with an authoritative major sound, while the last movement uses an energetic minor sound. Biehl sets the second movement apart by using the relative major key of C major, to create a serene atmosphere.

Sonatina in F Major (Anh. 5, No. 2), by Ludwig van Beethoven (1770-1827)

Beethoven was a very prolific composer, having written in nearly every genre from symphonies and large choral works to Lieder, instrumental chamber compositions, and piano pieces. He often associated certain moods with specific keys. This sonatina is written in F major, the same key as his spacious *Sixth Symphony (Pastorale)*. In this symphony, Beethoven uses the sounds of the orchestra to evoke country scenes—from imagery of the people to landscape and nature. We can use his symphony as an inspiration as we infuse feeling and emotion into this two-movement sonatina. Both the *Allegro assai* and the *Rondo* are in $\frac{2}{4}$ meter, but they are quite different in character.

Sonatina No. 6 in D Minor, by Georg Benda (1722-1795)

Georg Benda was born in Bohemia into a musical family. Throughout his lifetime he enjoyed success as a composer, violinist, and Kapellmeister, specializing in religious music. In addition to writing operas, he contributed significantly to the development of the *melodrama* (a musical stage-work that differs from opera since it includes spoken dramatic action accompanied by music). His tendency for dramatic development can be seen in this sonatina. It begins with fire—a scale rushing upwards followed by robust rising intervals. To create a more engaging and exciting performance, make the most of sudden contrasts of dynamics, articulations, rhythms, and phrasing.

Sonatina in C Major (Opus 55, No. 1), by Friedrich Kuhlau (1786-1832)

Friedrich Kuhlau was a German-born composer and pianist. He was introduced to music at an early age, since his father was a musician in a military band. He showed great talent and by 1804 was established as a concert pianist. In 1810, Kuhlau moved to Denmark and quickly gained a reputation as a pianist, teacher, and composer. Both movements of this sonatina go beyond the standard three-movement form. The first movement is fast and spirited, but Kuhlau indicates early on that it is to be played *dolce* (sweetly). The second movement should be played cheerfully, yet with grace. Paying close attention to the combinations of *legato* and *staccato* markings help create an elegant and nimble flow.

Sonatina (Opus 136, No. 4), by Carl Reinecke (1824-1910)

Carl Reinecke was a German composer, teacher, pianist, and conductor. He composed instrumental music and opera, but is perhaps best known for his piano works. Reinecke's compositions combine classical ideals with romantic spirit. The *Allegro moderato* makes great use of the bass register, putting the first theme in the left hand. The feel of the *Mazurka* is emphasized with rolled chords on the second beat, giving it stronger emphasis and bringing life to this Polish dance form. Throughout the sonatina, Reinecke makes use of interesting harmonic shifts, especially between the parallel major and minor keys, notably in the final movement.

Sonatina in F Major (Opus 4, No. 2), by Heinrich Lichner (1829-1898)

Heinrich Lichner spent his life working as an organist and as director of a large choral society. In his spare time, he was constantly inspired to write imaginative pedagogical pieces. Many of his compositions are brief character studies. His sonatinas for piano, especially Opp. 4, 49, and 66, are classical in style, but like Reinecke, his harmonies show the influence of romanticism. Both the first and second movements of this sonatina are tranquil and expressive, while the third movement contains the most fire. Strive to play the final *Rondo Polonaise* not only with robust exuberance, but also with a graceful fluidity.

Sonatina in G Major (Opus 20, No. 1), by Jan Ladislav Dussek (1760-1812)

Jan Ladislav Dussek was a Czech composer and pianist. He began music studies with his mother (a harpist and pianist) and his father (a well-known composer and organist). Dussek became a dazzling soloist. It was said that he was the first pianist to sit at the piano with his profile to the audience. The first movement begins with a fanfare opening, full of strength, with right-hand sixths accompanied by sonorous octaves. The second movement contrasts with a lovely, carefree melody. However, the character changes dramatically in the middle *minore* section, with more aggressive and mysterious sounds.

It.	- Italian
L.	- Latin
Abbr.	- Abbreviated

Dictionary

Tempo markings:	*Lento* – slow
	Andante – walking speed
	Andantino – slightly faster than *Andante*
	Allegretto – a little slower than *Allegro*
	Allegro – happy, spirited
	Vivace – lively and vivacious

a tempo — [It.] Return to the original tempo.

ad libitum   *ad lib.* — [L.} "At liberty" - indicating freedom in the performance (usually with tempo and dynamics)

Alberti bass — Accompaniment pattern consisting of broken chords with the notes of the pattern in the following order: low, high, middle, high; commonly found in the left hand of piano music.

allargando — [It.] Gradually slower and (usually) louder.

articulation — The proper and clear playing of *staccato, legato,* and phrasing.

assai — [It.] Very.

cantabile — [It.] In a singing manner.

compound meter — A time signature that can be divided into smaller meters. For example, $\frac{6}{8}$ meter can be divided into $\frac{3}{8}$ meter; $\frac{6}{2}$ meter can be divided into $\frac{2}{2}$.

con grazia — [It.] With grace.

con forza — [It.] With force.

D.C. al Fine — [It.] *Da capo al fine* - (Repeat) from the beginning to the end *(Fine)*.

dolce — [It.} "Sweetly" - to play with a softer, sweeter tone.

espressivo   *espr.* — [It.] "Expressively" - to play with much feeling and sentiment.

giocoso — [It.] Humorous, playful.

mazurka — A Polish folk dance, usually in $\frac{3}{4}$ meter.

minuet — A French dance in $\frac{3}{4}$ meter, usually in binary form, but also can include a Trio section, resulting in ternary (three-part) form.

misterioso		[It.] Mysteriously.
molto		[It.] Much, very.
non tanto		[It.] Not so much, not too much.
poco a poco		[It.] Little by little.
polonaise		A stately Polish dance in $\frac{3}{4}$ meter.
portato		[It.] Halfway between *legato* and *staccato*; indicated by *staccato* marks within a slur.
risoluto		[It.] "Resolved" - play in a determined, confident manner.
scherzo		[It.] A quick composition in triple mater, humorous and playful.
sempre		[It.] Always.
sentito		[It.] In a sincere and expressive manner.
senza		[It.] Without. *senza ritardando* - without getting slower.
simile	*sim.*	[It.] (Repeat) in a similar way.
sforzando	*sfz*	[It.] "Forcing" - with a strong, accented tone.
sostenuto	*sos.*	[It.] Sustained.
sotto voce		[It.] "Below and voice" - in an undertone; subdued.
subito	*sub.*	[It.] Suddenly.
tranquillo		[It.] Tranquil, calm.
tre corde	*t.c.*	[It.] A direction to lift the *una corda* pedal. (See definition below.)
una corda	*u.c.*	[It.] The leftmost pedal on the piano, often referred to as the "soft" pedal, since the hammers shift, hitting only 2 of the 3 unison strings and creating a gentler sound.

FJH PIANIST CURRICULUM CORRELATION CHART

The All-In-One Approach to Succeeding at the Piano®	Succeeding at the Piano®	Succeeding with a Notespeller	Succeeding with the Masters® (Baroque, Classical, Romantic Eras)	Succeeding with the Masters® Student Activity Books	The Festival Collection®	Succeeding with the Masters® The Festival Collection®* Etudes with Technique	Succeeding with the Masters®/ The Festival Collection® Sonatinas
Preparatory A and B	2nd Edition Preparatory Level	Preparatory (2nd edition coming in 2018)					
Books 1A and 1B	2nd Edition Grade 1A Grade 1B	Grade 1 (2nd edition coming in 2018)					
Books 2A and 2B	Grade 2A	Grade 2A (2nd edition coming in 2018)			Preparatory (Early Elementary through Mid-Elementary)	Preparatory (Early Elementary through Mid-Elem.)	
Book 2C	Grade 2B	Grade 2B (2nd edition coming in 2018)	On Your Way to Succeeding with the Masters® (Elementary through Late Elementary) with Theory Book		Book 1 (Elementary to Mid-Elementary)	Book 1 (Elementary to Mid-Elementary)	Book 1 (Mid-Elementary)
	Grade 3		An Introduction to Succeeding with the Masters® (Late Elementary through Intermediate) (Begin) Succeeding with the Masters®, Volume One (Late Elementary through Intermediate)	Student Activity Book Baroque Era, Volume One Classical Era, Volume One Teacher's Handbook Baroque Era, Volume One Classical Era, Volume One	Book 2 (Late Elementary)	Book 2 (Late Elementary)	Book 2 (Late Elementary to Early Intermediate)
	Grade 4		Succeeding with the Masters® Volume One (Late Elementary through Intermediate)	Student Activity Book and Teacher's Handbook Baroque Era, Volume One Classical Era, Volume One	Book 3 (Early Intermediate)	Book 3 (Early Intermediate)	Book 2 (Late Elementary to Early Int.)
	Grade 5		Succeeding with the Masters® Volume One (Late Elementary through Intermediate)	Student Activity Book and Teacher's Handbook Baroque Era, Volume One Classical Era, Volume One	Books 3 and 4 (Early Intermediate / Intermediate)	Books 3 and 4 (Early Intermediate / Intermediate)	Book 3 (Intermediate) Book 4 (Int. to Late Int.)
	Grade 5		Succeeding with the Masters® Volume One (Late Elementary through Intermediate)	Student Activity Book and Teacher's Handbook Baroque Era, Volume One Classical Era, Volume One	Books 3 and 4 (Early Intermediate / Int.)	Books 3 and 4 (Early Intermediate / Intermediate)	Book 3 (Intermediate) Book 4 (Int. to Late Int.)
	The Original core method consists of the same levels as the 2nd edition (Prep through Grade 5), except that Grade 1 is not separated into 1A and 1B. The Prep, 1, 2A, and 2B Original core levels are faster-paced with more technique and intervallic reading, discovery learning, more position changes, and pieces in different keys.		Succeeding with the Masters® Volume Two (Intermediate through Early Advanced)	Student Activity Book and Teacher's Handbook Baroque Era, Volume Two	Book 4 (Intermediate)	Book 4 (Intermediate)	Book 4 (Intermediate to Late Intermediate)
			Succeeding with the Masters® Volume Two (Intermediate through Early Advanced)	Student Activity Book and Teacher's Handbook Baroque Era, Volume Two	Book 5 (Late Intermediate)	Book 5 (Late Intermediate)	
			Succeeding with the Masters® Volume Two (Intermediate through Early Advanced)	Student Activity Book and Teacher's Handbook Baroque Volume Two	Book 6 (Late Int. to Early Advanced)		
					Book 7 (Early Advanced) and Book 8 (Advanced)	Book 8 will complete this series.	Book 6 will complete this series.

* *Succeeding with the Masters*® & *The Festival Collection*® *Teacher's Handbook* correlates the repertoire between these two series.

FJH PIANIST CURRICULUM CORRELATION CHART

The In Recital® Series**	Sight Reading & Rhythm Every Day®	Write, Play, and Hear Your Theory Every Day®	Energize Your Fingers Every Day®	Intervallic Reading Series	Play Your Scales & Chords Every Day®	The FJH Contemporary Keyboard Editions
In Recital®Ready, Set, Play! In Recital® with Little Pieces for Little Fingers			Preparatory			
Book 1 (Early Elementary)	Books A & B "Let's Get Started!" Books 1A & 1B	Book 1	Book 1	Be A Star! Book 1 (Early Elementary/Elementary) Be A Star at Christmas! (Elementary to Late Elementary) On Stage! Book 1 (Early Elementary/Elementary) Be A Star! Hymns, Book 1 (Early Elementary to Elementary)	Book 1	
Book 2 (Elementary)	Book 2A	Book 2	Book 2A	Be A Star! Book 2 (Late Elementary) Be A Star! Hymns, Book 2 (Late Elementary) On Stage! Book 2 (Elementary/Late Elementary)	Book 1	Contemporary Collage, Volume 1, Book 1 Pictures and Beyond, Book 1
Book 3 (Late Elementary)	Book 2B	Book 3	Book 2B	Be A Star! Book 2 (Late Elementary) On Stage! Book 2 (Elementary/Late Elementary)	Book 2	Contemporary Collage, Volume 1, Book 1
Book 3 (Late Elementary)	Book 3A	Book 4	Book 3 (2018)	Be A Star! Book 3 (Early Intermediate to Mid-Int.) On Stage! Book 3 (Early Intermediate/Intermediate) Be A Star! Book 3 (Early Intermediate to Mid-Int.) On Stage! Book 3 (Early Intermediate/Intermediate)	Book 3 Book 4 (2018)	Echoes, Pictures, Riddles, and Tales for Piano Solo
Book 4 (Early Intermediate)	Book 3B	Book 4	Book 4 (2018)			Echoes, Pictures, Riddles, and Tales for Piano Solo Travels Through Sound
Books 4 and 5 (Early Intermediate/Intermediate)	Book 4A	Book 5				Modern Miniatures, Volume 1 Contemporary Collage Volume 1, Book 2
Book 5 (Intermediate)	Book 4B	Book 5				SOUND/WORLD, Vol. 1 Reaching Out, for Solo Piano Portraits for Piano
Book 6 (Late Intermediate)	Book 5	Book 5				Contemporary Collage, Volume 1, Book 3 Musical Treasures, Vol. 1
Book 6 (Late Intermediate)	Book 6	Book 6				Musical Treasures, Vol. 2 Outside the Box Watercolors for Ten Fingers
In Recital® for the Advancing Pianist*** (Early Advanced)	Book 6	Book 6				Concertino No. 1 Preludes, Volume 1
	Books 7 and 8	Book 7 (2018)	Book 6 will complete this series.		Book 5 will complete this series.	SOUND/WORLD, Vol. 2 Modern Miniatures, Vol. 2 Piano Album**** Modern Expressions for Piano

** Includes: *In Recital® Throughout the Year, Volumes One* and *Two; Christmas Favorites; Duets; Classical Themes; Jazz, Blues, & Rags; Popular Christmas Music; Popular Music; All-Time Favorites; Timeless Hymns;* and *The Best of In Recital Solos®*.

*** Includes: *In Recital® for the Advancing Pianist—Christmas; Popular Christmas; Jazz & Blues; Original Solos, Book 1; Popular, Books 1 and 2; Classical Themes;* and *Duets*.

**** *The FJH Contemporary Keyboard Editions* contain many more publications from elementary to advanced levels. A catalog for the complete series is available upon request.

FJH2204